D1116713

RAMPS

THE COOKBOOK

Cooking with the Best Kept Secret of the Appalachian Trail

RAMPS

THE COOKBOOK

Cooking with the Best Kept Secret of the Appalachian Trail

Compiled by
the Editors of St. Lynn's Press

st. lynn's
press

Pittsburgh, PA

RAMPS
Cooking with the Best Kept Secret of the Appalachian Trail
Copyright © 2012 St. Lynn's Press

ISBN-13: 978-0-9832726-2-5

Library of Congress Control Number: 2011943347
CIP information available upon request

First Edition, 2012

St. Lynn's Press . POB 18680 . Pittsburgh, PA 15236
412.466.0790 • www.stlynnspress.com

Typesetting and cover design – Holly Rosborough, Network Printing Services
Front Cover photograph – ©Eve Fox
Back Cover photograph – ©Justin Kern
Editor–Catherine Dees

Recipe photos and text-related photos are credited on their pages.
Additional photo credits: Welcome page, ©Howard Walfish;
From Woods to Kitchen page, ©Marielle Anzelone; p. 4, ©Herban Feast Catering;
p. 13, ©Maggie Raptis; p.81 ©Darya Pino; p.98, ©Joel MacCharles.
Ramp illustration used throughout interior and on back cover, ©J-P Thimot.

*Disclaimer: The publisher expressly disclaims any responsibility for any adverse effects
occurring as a result of the suggestions or information herein, including the
handling or consuming of plants named in this book.*

Printed in The United States of America on triple-certified FSC, SFI, and PEFC paper

This title and all of St. Lynn's Press books may be purchased for educational,
business, or sales promotional use. For information please write:
Special Markets Department . St. Lynn's Press . POB 18680 . Pittsburgh, PA 15236

10 9 8 7 6 5 4 3 2 1

WELCOME TO THE WIDE WORLD OF RAMPS!

*I*n these pages we have brought together a truly special collection of ramp recipes. They represent traditional Appalachian dishes handed down through the generations as well as modern takes on this aromatic spring delicacy, created by adventurous chefs, food writers and bloggers across North America – from Toronto to Florida, New York to Oregon and points in between. In the Great Lakes region ramps are better known as wild leeks, but whatever the name, the enjoyment is the same.

We wish you many happy moments exploring the earthy delights of ramps at your table.

The Editors

TABLE OF CONTENTS

Foreword.. i
Introduction v
From Woods to Kitchen.. 1

Recipes

Sides & Main Dishes 5
Pickled Ramps.. 6
Caramelized Ramps.. 8
Sweet & Sour Ramps... 10
Grilled Tuna with Ramps....................................... 12
Little Neck Clams with Ramps & Asparagus.................... 14
One-hour Calamari in Umido with Ramp Bruschetta............ 16
Parsnip, Red Bell Pepper & Ramp Burritos..................... 18
Chicken Braised in White Wine & Ramps 20
Ramp Porcupine Meatballs.................................... 22
Ramps & Red Potatoes... 23
Ramp, Potato, Spinach Gratin 24
Wok-Braised Ramps 26
Roasted Fish Wrapped in Ramps............................... 28
Wild Ramp Lemon Risotto..................................... 30
Quinoa Pilaf with Ramps, Artichokes & Peas................... 32
Spring Vegetable Curry with Ramp Cilantro Chutney............ 34

Salads & Soups... 37
Ramp Green Goddess Dressing 38
Ramp Ranch Dressing.. 40
Shaved Asparagus & Ramp Salad.............................. 42
Dandelion Greens Salad with Ramps, Bacon & Blue Cheese.......... 44
Chickpea & Spring Green Salad 46
Crema of Ramps with Wild Asparagus 48
Easy Mixed Bean & Ramp Soup 50
Ramp Udon Soup 52
The L Train Ramp Soup 56

Ramps & Eggs 61

Buckwheat Crêpes with Egg, Ramps & Bacon.............................. 62
Eggs with Ramps & Bacon... 64
Risotto Cake with Crispy Ramps (and a Fried Egg) 66
Ramps, Morels & Fresh Peas with Poached Eggs.......................... 68
Spring Vegetable Frittata 70

Biscuits & Muffins, Etc. 73

Ramp Pesto Cornmeal Muffins 74
Buttermilk Ramp Biscuits (1)... 76
Buttermilk Ramp Biscuits (2)... 78
Ramp Fritters... 80
Sweet Corn Griddle Cakes 82

Sauces, Dips, Etc. 85

Spicy Ramp Cheese Dip 86
Simple Crab/Ramp Dip.. 87
Ramp & Arugula Pesto 88
Ramps Mayonnaise... 90
Ramp Hummus 92

Juice & Jam 93

Delightful Ramp Twist 94
Dot Montgillion's Ramp Jam 96

Year-Round Ramps.. 99

A "Nose-to-Tail" Approach to Preserving Ramps........................ 100
Dehydrating: Ramp Roots 102
Drying: Salt & Vinegar-Style Ramp Chips 102
Infusing: Ramp-infused Sherry Vinegar................................ 104
Freezing: Basic Pesto 104

Ramp Festivals and Other Events 106

Sources That Will Ship Ramps To You............................ 110

Acknowledgments.. 112

Foreword

I was honored when I was asked to write the foreword to this book. Since opening our first restaurant more than a decade ago, my wife Ellen Kassoff and I have been passionate advocates for regionality and seasonality on the plate.

The relationships Ellen and I have formed with local farmers over the years have cemented our dedication to the movement. These are not only our great friends but essential business partners too. Local farmers dictate our menu. When seasonal ingredients are available we use 'em!

Which brings me to a special favorite of ours: Ramps – one of the great culinary harbingers of spring. This wild-foraged relative of the leek has unique, versatile qualities that can't be found in any other vegetable.

Over the years I have used ramps in many of my recipes. It has become a staple on my spring seasonal menus, and I'm pleased to note its increasing and well-deserved popularity. Ramps have a growing following with innovative chefs all over North America who are introducing this unique Appalachian treasure to a wider audience.

The ramp's short season makes it that much more cherished. As eagerly as I seek it out each spring, I'm also aware that it has become endangered in some areas, and foragers need to be sensitive to that reality. It's important to the future of this delight to be aware of its vulnerability to over-foraging. We obtain our ramps only from sources who use sustainable foraging practices.

We can't overstate the value of building a closer sense of community among chefs and local farmers – and between the general public and their local farmers' markets. There is so much good that comes from a shared passion for fresh, local, seasonal foods. Ellen and I are grateful to be able to play a part in inspiring a deeper appreciation of the simple pleasures growing all around us.

Which brings me back to ramps. A cookbook devoted solely to ramp recipes is long overdue. We are delighted that this talented group of chefs and writers has come together to offer a wide selection of their best for your pleasure. Enjoy!

Todd C. Gray

Chef and co-owner of
Equinox and Watershed restaurants
in Washington, D. C.

INTRODUCTION

*T*he ramp (Allium tricoccum) *is a wild herb that flourishes in the shade of hardwood forests. It is nurtured by the leafy mulch, which also provides consistent moisture. Unlike other alliums – garlic, onions, leeks, chives – it has a broad leaf one to two inches wide and ten to twelve inches long, as opposed to a tube. Its taste is somewhere between a garlic and an onion, except that it doesn't have a sharp bite and it doesn't make you cry. It has a rich taste, not like anything else, and it lingers long after the last morsel has been eaten.*

Ramps are found throughout the Appalachian region and much of the northeastern United States, extending into Canada and as far west as Wisconsin. A slightly different variety of ramp can be found in Europe, Japan and the Far East. Ramps make their brief appearance in spring, when ramp diggers descend on the woods in search of this pungent treat.

Hello, I'm Glen Facemire, Jr., and I was raised in the mountains of West Virginia. I have had the privilege of having ramps on my table for some 60 years. My mother would cold pack the ramps in half-gallon jars to last us through the winter. When spring arrived we would start all over and enjoy the fresh ramps, along with poke greens, fiddlehead ferns and mushrooms. Where I was raised, the logging camps in the spring of the year always had an air about them that was the aroma of ramps cooking. The cook would put them in fried potatoes for dinner and serve them with scrambled eggs for breakfast.

Ramps for me and many of my peers growing up was not something so special, it was just a wild herb that most folks were fond of eating. It was always part of our lives. Foraging for it was a way to make a few dollars for spending money. As I grew older, I developed a deeper understanding of this wonderful plant.

Wherever the ramp *(Allium tricoccum)* appears, you find those who have discovered the unique flavor as well as the health claims that go with them. High in minerals and vitamins A and C, the ramp is appreciated as a blood cleanser and has been called one of the best spring tonics to be found. Many people will testify to a calming and relaxed feeling after eating ramps. Medical research into the ramp's possible cancer benefits has been published in the Linus Pauling Institute of Medical Study and is ongoing. Whatever it is that the ramp has, it has stood the test of time and is still going strong in the kitchens of some of the most popular chefs throughout the United States and Canada.

Ramp dinners and festivals are the talk of the town throughout Appalachia in April and early May. Some people will travel several hundred miles to have what we call a "mess of ramps." They are quite often served with brown beans, fried potatoes, corn bread, ham or bacon, buttermilk or sassafras tea.

Richwood, West Virginia, is known as The Ramp Capital of the World and has laid claim to the title for over 50 years. The ramp cleaning starts about a week before the big Richwood ramp feed and is not finished until about a ton of ramps have been cleaned and put in the cooler for that big day, the third weekend in April.

Many folks have been introduced to the special appeal of ramps through these festivals, some as small as a family get together or a fund-raiser for a fire department. These dinners and festivals, ranging from ten or 15 people to over a thousand, have ushered in an increased interest in ramps, which in turn has stressed the wild patches to the extent that some areas have banned the digging of ramps altogether and have put limits on the amount of ramps that can be harvested.

I have spent much of my life studying the ramp as a naturalist with a passion for this herb of the wild. At my West Virginia farm I have sought to ensure the future enjoyment of ramps for those who come after us by promoting sustainable cultivation through seed and bulb preservation. I am pleased to report that in the last 15 years or so ramp seeds and ramp bulbs have been introduced to family herb gardens in areas where there were only small amounts of ramps or in some cases no ramps left in the wild at all — a very hopeful sign.

A better understanding of the ramp and ramp growing has come to the general population through books, lectures and online web sites. I also give credit to the Small Farms Bureau and timber management areas for aiding in the preservation of the ramp and its responsible harvesting.

It is my opinion that with a little help the ramp will be with us for many, many years to come, to grace our tables and to give us family and community get-togethers for fun and fundraising for worthy causes.

May you enjoy the recipes that have been prepared for us with that most unique herb, the ramp.

Glen Facemire, Jr.
The Ramp Farm
Richwood, West Virginia

Editor's Note: Glen Facemire, Jr., and his wife Noreen are the proprietors of the Ramp Farm. In his book, *Having Your Ramps and Eating Them Too,* he has put together his lifetime's passion for, and knowledge of, ramps. For more information visit www.rampfarm.com.

From Woods
to Kitchen

Many ramp foragers have their secret spots they return to year after year. We follow one forager to his secret ramp patch somewhere in the Hudson Valley.

Ramps emerging from thick, leafy mulch

Likely candidates

Digging with care

Bulb, stem and leaf exposed

PHOTOS BY **CHRISTOPHER MATTHEWS**

Hours later, in a New York City kitchen: cleaning and trimming

Ready for the cook

PHOTOS BY **KATHRYN MATTHEWS**

Ramps out west: at a Seattle-area farmers' market

Sides & Main Dishes

PICKLED RAMPS

Yields 1 quart

Special equipment: canning jar

❧ INGREDIENTS

1 pound ramps, washed well, ends trimmed
1½ cups white wine vinegar or rice vinegar
1½ cups water
1½ cups sugar
¼ cup salt
3 bay leaves
1 tablespoon yellow or black mustard seed
6 allspice berries
Pinch red pepper flakes

❧ DIRECTIONS

Carefully pack ramps into a sterilized quart-sized jar with a seal-on or screw-top lid.

Combine remaining ingredients in a medium saucepan over medium-high heat and bring to a boil, whisking until sugar and salt are dissolved. Pour hot brine over ramps (it should fill the jar completely; if you have excess, discard). Seal or screw on lid and allow to cool at room temperature. Transfer to refrigerator and allow to rest for at least 3 weeks, and up to a year, before consuming.

RECIPE AND PHOTO BY **KENJI LOPEZ-ALT**, *SERIOUS EATS* BLOG
(WWW.SERIOUSEATS.COM)

CARAMELIZED RAMPS

Serves 4–6 as a side dish

INGREDIENTS

3 tablespoons unsalted butter
2 pounds ramp bulbs, fresh or frozen
3 tablespoons turbinado sugar
  (brown sugar may be substituted)
1 teaspoon salt
¼ teaspoon freshly ground black pepper
3 tablespoons balsamic vinegar
1 tablespoon chopped fresh parsley

DIRECTIONS

Preheat the oven to 400°F.

Melt butter in an ovenproof sauté pan over medium heat. The pan should be large enough to hold all the ramp bulbs in a single layer. Add bulbs and cook until they begin to brown slightly, about 10 minutes. Add sugar and toss, continuing to cook until sugar melts and begins to bubble, about 2 minutes. Add salt, pepper and vinegar and cook for 5 minutes longer.

Place the pan in the oven, uncovered, and roast for 15 minutes. Remove to a serving dish and sprinkle with chopped parsley. Serve while still warm.

RECIPE AND PHOTO BY **DAVID EGER**, *EARTHY DELIGHTS* BLOG
(WWW.EARTHYDELIGHTSBLOG.COM)

SWEET & SOUR RAMPS

Serves 4 as a side dish

☙ INGREDIENTS

2–3 dozen young ramps
3 tablespoons olive oil
3 tablespoons white wine or sherry vinegar
3 tablespoons light-colored honey
Freshly ground black pepper for garnish

☙ DIRECTIONS

Clean the ramps and remove the leaves or green parts (use them for another recipe).

Sauté the ramps in olive oil over medium-high heat until they brown, about 5 minutes.

Add vinegar and honey and swirl to combine in the pan. Turn the heat down and simmer until the liquid reduces to a glaze, about another 3-5 minutes.

Serve hot or at room temperature with black pepper to taste.

RECIPE AND PHOTO BY **HANK SHAW**, *HUNTER ANGLER GARDENER COOK* BLOG
(WWW.HONEST-FOOD.NET)

GRILLED TUNA WITH RAMPS, ANASAZI BEANS & CHARRED TOMATO VINAIGRETTE

Serves 4

INGREDIENTS

½ cup Anasazi beans, pre-soaked for at least 2 hours
2 tablespoons salt, divided
4 Roma tomatoes
3 teaspoons freshly ground black pepper, divided
1 cup extra virgin olive oil
4 tuna steaks, about 1 inch thick
8 fresh ramps
1 tablespoon rice wine vinegar
1 tablespoon fresh parsley

DIRECTIONS

Preheat grill to high.

In a saucepan, add one quart cold water and the pre-soaked beans. Simmer over medium heat for about 1 hour. After 30 minutes, add ½ tablespoon of the salt. After 45 minutes, check for doneness. They should be soft but with just a slight bite to them. Remove from heat and drain. If not used immediately chill in ice water and reserve.

Toss tomatoes in ½ tablespoon of the salt, 1 teaspoon of the pepper, and ¼ cup of the olive oil. Grill over high heat, turning often until charred all the way around. Remove from heat and cover in a bowl until soft all the way through.

Combine tomatoes, vinegar, ½ tablespoon of the salt, 1 teaspoon of the pepper in a food processor and purée. Slowly add all but one tablespoon of the olive oil until well incorporated. Adjust the seasonings and reserve.

Rub the tuna steaks and the ramps with the remaining olive oil, salt and pepper and grill the tuna for only about 2 minutes per side. The ramps should be grilled for about the same time, or until soft.

To serve: Place a mound of the (warm) beans in the center of four plates. Slice the tuna into about 5 slices and fan over the beans. Drizzle the vinaigrette around the plate and top everything with two grilled ramps on each plate.

RECIPE BY **CHEF CHRIS PERKEY**, IRON RESTAURANT, GRAND RAPIDS, MI

LITTLE NECK CLAMS WITH RAMPS & ASPARAGUS

I was so excited to find good looking asparagus and clams at the grocery, but I was even more excited to find some wild ramps! I have had the hardest time locating this treat, mainly because we don't live terribly close to the farmers' market and by the time I wake up and get there, they are all gone. I love their garlicky flavor and smooth texture. I decided to combine them all to make one simple, really fresh, super spring-like dish. It was so, so good. I served it with some crusty bread and it was the perfect early April meal.

Serves 4

❧ INGREDIENTS

2 pounds little neck clams (about 50)
1 pound asparagus, cut into 2-inch pieces
1¼ cup chopped wild ramps
1 cup dry white wine or stock
3 tablespoons minced Italian parsley
1 tablespoon olive oil

❧ DIRECTIONS

In a heavy pot with a lid, sauté the ramps and asparagus for about 2 minutes in the oil. Add the clams and wine. Cover and bring to a boil. Reduce heat and steam until the clams have opened, about 3 minutes. Discard any unopened clams.

RECIPE AND PHOTO BY **RACHEL RAPPAPORT**, *COCONUT & LIME* BLOG
(WWW.COCONUTANDLIME.COM)

ONE-HOUR CALAMARI IN UMIDO WITH RAMP BRUSCHETTA

Serves 4

INGREDIENTS

3 pounds cleaned calamari
½ cup extra-virgin olive oil
10 garlic cloves, peeled and left whole
1 tablespoon hot red pepper flakes
1 cup dry white wine
2 cups Basic Tomato Sauce (recipe below)
2 bunches ramps (about 16 ramps), cleaned
1 bunch marjoram, leaves only
Salt and pepper
4 thick slices Italian peasant bread

DIRECTIONS

Check the calamari for any cartilage and cut into 1-inch pieces. Place the calamari in a 6-quart saucepan, add ¼ cup of the olive oil, the garlic, red pepper flakes, wine, and tomato sauce, and bring to a boil. Lower the heat to a rapid simmer and cook 1 hour.

Preheat the grill or broiler.

Grill the ramps until wilted, about 1 minute. Set aside to cool, then chop the cooled ramps into ½-inch pieces. Place in a mixing bowl with remaining ¼ cup olive oil and the marjoram leaves and stir to blend. Keep grill hot.

When the calamari is tender, season with salt and pepper. Toast the bread on the grill. Spoon the ramp mixture over the bread, divide the calamari among 4 bowls, top each with a bruschetta, and serve.

BASIC TOMATO SAUCE
Makes 4 cups

¼ cup extra-virgin olive oil
1 large onion, cut in ¼-inch dice
4 garlic cloves, thinly sliced
3 tablespoons chopped fresh thyme leaves,
   or 1 tablespoon dried
½ medium carrot, finely shredded
2 (28-ounce) cans peeled whole tomatoes,
   crushed by hand and juices reserved
Kosher salt to taste

In a 3-quart saucepan, heat the olive oil over medium heat, add the onion and garlic and cook until soft and light golden brown, 8-10 minutes. Add the thyme and carrot and cook 5 minutes more, until the carrot is quite soft. Add the tomatoes and juice and bring to a boil, stirring often.

Lower the heat and simmer for 30 minutes until as thick as hot cereal. Season with salt. This sauce holds 1 week in the refrigerator or up to 6 months in the freezer.

RECIPE BY **MARIO BATALI**, FROM *SIMPLE ITALIAN FOOD* (CLARKSON POTTER 1998)
(WWW.MARIOBATALI.COM)

PARSNIP, RED BELL PEPPER & RAMP BURRITOS

This is a completely non-traditional burrito filling – a perfectly sane way to celebrate Cinco de Mayo when you are an Italian girl who didn't taste her first Mexican food until she was old enough to be legally wed.

Serves 2

INGREDIENTS

2 teaspoons olive oil
1 medium-large parsnip, peeled and diced
4–5 ramps, white parts only
   (can substitute scallions or green onions)
¼ red bell pepper, diced
Pinch of salt, and to taste
½ cup white beans (or any bean that you have on hand)
½ cup asparagus, sliced on a diagonal
¼–½ teaspoon smoked paprika
¼ teaspoon chipotle chili powder
2 burrito-sized flour tortillas

DIRECTIONS

In a large skillet, heat the olive oil over medium heat. Add in the parsnip, ramps and bell pepper with a pinch of salt (this helps to caramelize the veggies). Sauté for 4 minutes, stirring occasionally. Add in the white beans, asparagus, smoked paprika and chili powder. Stir mixture until all veggies are coated, then cover the pan and allow to cook for another 4–5 minutes, or until the parsnips are fork-tender. Add salt to taste.

When the filling is done, heat a medium-sized non-stick skillet over medium heat and heat the tortillas, one at a time, for 30 seconds on each side. Remove to a plate. Place half the filling in the center of each burrito so that it forms a nice compact rectangle in the center. Fold one edge over the filling. Tuck in the left and right sides and then continue to roll the burrito towards the unfolded edge until it's sealed.

RECIPE AND PHOTO BY **JOANNE BRUNO**, *EATS WELL WITH OTHERS* BLOG
(WWW.JOANNE-EATSWELLWITHOTHERS.COM)

CHICKEN BRAISED IN
WHITE WINE & RAMPS

This is an easily adaptable recipe. The method was inspired by Jamie Oliver. When ramps are not in season, try shallots with fresh sage, or tiny cippolini onions with thyme or summer savory; green garlic would also work nicely.

Serves 4

❧ INGREDIENTS

    1 roaster chicken (3–4 pounds), preferably sustainably raised
    1 teaspoon coarse salt
    1 teaspoon freshly ground black pepper
    1 bunch ramps, washed and root ends trimmed
       (about 15–20 ramps)
    3 tablespoons olive oil
    3 tablespoons butter
    1 cup white wine (I used a local Chardonnay, Duet,
       from Hopkins Vineyards)
    1 cup chicken stock
    6 large cloves garlic
    Zest and juice from 1 lemon

❧ DIRECTIONS

Wash the chicken, inside and out, under lukewarm running water and dry thoroughly with paper towels (or a clean kitchen towel). Sprinkle with salt and pepper. Allow to dry, unwrapped, in the refrigerator if you have the time; otherwise, allow to sit at room temperature, uncovered, for at least 30 minutes to warm the bird prior to cooking.

Preheat the oven to 375°F (350°F convection).

Chop ramp bulbs into ½-inch pieces. Separate the ramp leaves, stack about 10 leaves on top of each other, roll into a tight cigar, and slice into ¼-inch ribbons. Repeat with remaining ramp leaves. Stuff the cavity of the chicken with 2 or 3 bulbs and a small handful of leaves.

Heat olive oil and butter over medium-high heat in a Dutch oven or casserole with a tight-fitting lid, one that will fit the chicken snugly. Heat until the butter foam subsides and the oil is shimmering, but not smoking. Add the chicken and fry, turning on all sides, until the skin is crispy and golden, about 10–15 minutes (I find that using 2 sturdy wooden spatulas to turn the chicken is the easiest way to do it without tearing the skin).

Once the skin is nicely browned, remove the chicken to a plate, and pour off all but 3 tablespoons of the fat. Add the wine and scrape the browned bits off the bottom of the pan. Return the chicken to the pan; add the stock, ramps, garlic, lemon juice and zest. Roast, covered, in the preheated oven for approximately 1 hour (45 minutes convection), or until the internal temperature is at least 165°F. Remove the lid, raise the oven temperature to broil, and crisp the chicken skin lightly, for about 3–4 minutes. Remove the pot from the oven, transfer the chicken to a cutting board, and tent under foil for at least 15 minutes. In the meantime, bring the sauce to a boil and reduce until it thickens and just starts to turn syrupy, about 10 minutes.

Carve and serve over couscous, rice or mashed potatoes. Top with hot reduction sauce, including plenty of ramps and garlic.

RECIPE BY **KAELA PORTER**, *LOCAL KITCHEN* BLOG
(WWW.LOCALKITCHENBLOG.COM)

RAMP PORCUPINE MEATBALLS

Makes 18 meatballs

🌿 INGREDIENTS

2 pounds ground beef
1 egg, beaten
½ cup milk
1 cup chopped ramps
⅔ cup rice, uncooked
1 teaspoon chili powder, plus 1 teaspoon*
2 teaspoons salt, plus 1 teaspoon
2½ cups tomatoes, fresh or canned
2½ cups water
2 tablespoons chopped onion

Chili powder may be omitted

🌿 DIRECTIONS

Mix together meat, egg, milk, ramps, rice, chili powder and 2 teaspoons salt. Form into 1½-inch balls. In a skillet, brown in hot fat.

In a large saucepan, combine tomatoes, water, onion and remaining seasonings. Bring to a boil, then drop meatballs in. Cover and cook slowly on low heat for 1½ hours.

RECIPE BY **GLEN FACEMIRE, JR.,** FROM
HAVING YOUR RAMPS AND EATING THEM TOO (McCLAIN 2008)

RAMPS & RED POTATOES

Want a really easy recipe for ramps and red potatoes? You've come to the right place! This recipe is a good starting point, but the more ramps you use with your potatoes, the better!

Serves 4-plus as a side dish

🍂 INGREDIENTS

1 large ramp
5 medium red potatoes
4 tablespoons olive oil
Dash garlic salt
Dash cayenne pepper
Dash paprika
Dash black pepper

🍂 DIRECTIONS

Thoroughly wash the ramp. Cut off the bulb root end. Cut off the stalks to the light greenish area. You may opt to use the inner-most stalks, too. Cut the ramp into ¼-inch pieces. Add olive oil to your frying pan and fry the ramp about 10 minutes on low heat.

Wash the potatoes and cut into bite-size cubes. Add to the ramp. Season with a dash of garlic salt, paprika, cayenne pepper (to suit your taste), and black pepper.

Cover and fry on a lower heat for up to 30 minutes. Stir occasionally to keep the potatoes from getting too brown.

RECIPE AND PHOTO BY **JULIE BRADY** (JAGUAR JULIE), *SQUIDOO* BLOG
(WWW.SQUIDOO.COM/LENSMASTERS/JAGUARJULIE)

RAMP, POTATO, SPINACH GRATIN WITH RACLETTE CHEESE

Remembering a leek and potato recipe I had seen from Melissa Clark, I decided to do a riff on that using ramps, spinach, and Raclette cheese. I wanted to keep it super simple to bring forth the pungent flavor of the ramps.

Serves 4–6

➣ INGREDIENTS

    2 tablespoons unsalted butter, plus more for greasing pan
    1 pound baby Yukon Gold potatoes, washed
    Salt and black pepper to taste
    2 bunches ramps (if unavailable, leeks can substitute)
    3 cups spinach
    ½ cup heavy cream
    1 garlic clove; minced finely
    A pinch of nutmeg
    ¼–½ cup Raclette cheese, shredded*

    *Raclette cheese is a good melting cheese that has a mild nutty
    flavor similar to a Fontina or Taleggio. Either of those would be
    great substitutes if you can't find Raclette.*

➣ DIRECTIONS

Preheat the oven to 350°F. Grease an oven-proof 1–quart (approximately) casserole dish with a dab of butter. Set aside.

Using a mandoline, thinly slice the potatoes and overlap them in the casserole dish. Season each layer generously with salt and pepper. You should have about 2 layers of potatoes.

In a medium saucepan set over medium-high heat, melt the 2 tablespoons of butter and let brown until it smells nutty and the foam has subsided a bit, about 1 minute. Meanwhile, roughly chop up the ramps and spinach, separating the bottom white ramp bulbs from the delicate greens. Toss the bulbs into the browned butter and sauté until softened, about 30 seconds. Add the rest of the ramps and spinach, stirring and sautéing until they wilt slightly, about another 30 seconds.

Spread the ramp and spinach butter mixture over the potatoes.

Using the same saucepan, add the cream, nutmeg and garlic, and simmer for approximately 3 minutes. Pour the mixture over the ramp, spinach and potatoes. Sprinkle shredded cheese over the top and cover with foil.

Bake for approximately 40 minutes, or until potatoes are fork tender.

RECIPE BY **STEPHANIE RUSSELL**, *OKIE DOKIE ARTICHOKIE* BLOG
(WWW.OKIEDOKIEARTICHOKIE.ME)

WOK-BRAISED RAMPS

We like ramps to shine in all their untamed, garlicky, green spring tonic glory. Which means no accompanying meat, fish or dairy. Just ramps.

INGREDIENTS

1 pound ramps, washed well, bulbs cleaned of dirt
1½ tablespoons extra-virgin olive oil
4–5 garlic cloves, minced
¼ cup water

DIRECTIONS

Separate white ramp bulbs from stalk and roughly chop.

Heat wok with olive oil over medium-high heat. When oil is hot but not smoking (a drop of water will sizzle in it), add chopped ramp bulbs. Sauté quickly, then lower heat to medium low. Sauté 2–3 minutes, or until the white bulbs soften and brown somewhat.

Add minced garlic and sauté until just incorporated. Add green leaves, raising heat to medium. Sauté until all the leaves wilt, about 2–3 minutes. Add ¼ cup water and stir quickly through ramps or garlic that may be sticking. Reduce heat to low (or simmer) and cover. Cook 8 minutes. Uncover, if there is any residual water, raise heat and continue stirring ramps until all the water has evaporated. Add kosher or sea salt, to taste. Serve.

Note: I use a flat-bottomed, well-seasoned wok. It's fast, easy and works well on either a gas range, which we have in the City (NYC), or on our (inherited) electric stove in the country (Hudson Valley). If you don't have a wok, try a sauté pan with deep sides, or a Dutch oven.

RECIPE AND PHOTO BY **KATHRYN MATTHEWS**, *UPSTATE-DOWNTOWN* BLOG
(WITH **CHRISTOPHER MATTHEWS**)
(UPSTATEDOWNTOWNNY.COM)

ROASTED FISH WRAPPED IN RAMPS

Here's a super simple recipe for roasted fish wrapped in ramps. It makes a colorful presentation when served with ramp pesto and a red wine sauce.

Number of servings depends on number of fish pieces used

⚬ INGREDIENTS

Ramp greens, washed (1 per piece of fish)
Cod, cut into 3-inch pieces, or slightly larger
Fresh lemon juice and fresh herbs, for garnish

⚬ DIRECTIONS

Blanch the ramp greens: Drop the leaves into boiling salt water and cook until tender. Plunge ramps into an ice bath to stop the cooking.

Wrap a leaf around each piece of cod and sauté the wrapped fish, being sure to not overcook the fish (it should be translucent in the center and more opaque on the outside)

Present the roasted, ramp-wrapped cod on a plate with a bit of ramp pesto* and a little red wine sauce. Drizzle with a little bit of fresh lemon juice and garnish with fresh herbs.

see ramp pesto recipes on pages 74, 88 and 104

RECIPE BY **CHEF BOB ADKINS**, FARMBLOOMINGTON RESTAURANT, BLOOMINGTON, IN
PHOTO BY **ALYCIN BEKTESH**

WILD RAMP LEMON RISOTTO

Serves 4

INGREDIENTS

1 quart vegetable stock
3 tablespoons unsalted butter, divided
1 cup sliced ramps, thoroughly cleaned and
   the white and green parts divided
1 cup carnaroli rice (arborio or another short-grained,
   stubby rice is fine as well)
¼ cup dry white wine
Juice and zest of 1 lemon
Parmesan Reggiano
Good salt and fresh black pepper

DIRECTIONS

In a small saucepan bring vegetable stock to a simmer (you'll be using this in just a few minutes). Place a heavy-bottomed, tall-sided pan or Dutch oven over medium heat and add 1 tablespoon butter and the sliced white portion of the ramps, and sweat for two minutes. This is akin to sweating an onion; you want translucency, not golden color.

Slightly increase the heat and add the rice, stirring frequently to completely coat the rice with the hot butter. Cook for a few minutes until the rice is no longer opaque. Cooking the risotto rice and ramps in this way adds texture and flavor to the final dish.

Add the wine to the rice and cook until it has completely evaporated. Lightly season the rice with salt, and then add enough hot stock to just barely cover the rice. Stir, letting the rice absorb

the liquid almost entirely before adding a small amount more. The rice should be cooking at a moderate temperature and slowly bubbling as you continue stirring and adding liquid. This will take about 15 minutes total. Taste the rice for doneness: it should have lost its "raw" crunch, but still be firm in the middle. Cook for a minute or two longer, then add the remaining butter, lemon zest and lemon juice.

Stir in the ramp greens and season the risotto with more salt and fresh black pepper. Adjust the consistency with a little more hot stock if necessary (the finished dish should be smoothly emulsified and pourable without being watery).

Finally, grate some Parmesan into the risotto and gently give it one or two stirs to incorporate the cheese without creating a stringy texture. Serve immediately.

RECIPE BY **CHEF TIMOTHY WASTELL**, FIREHOUSE RESTAURANT, PORTLAND, OR
PHOTO BY **HOLLY ROSBOROUGH**

QUINOA PILAF WITH RAMPS, ARTICHOKES & PEAS

Serves 6 as a main dish, 8 as a side dish

INGREDIENTS

1 bunch ramps (15 – 20 ramps)
Zest of 2 lemons, finely grated, plus juice of 1 lemon
2 tablespoons flat-leaf parsley, chopped
4 tablespoons extra virgin olive oil
1 lemon, halved
10 baby artichokes
3 cloves garlic, minced
½ teaspoon fresh thyme
2 cups quinoa, well rinsed (unless you use a pre-rinsed variety)
½ cup dry white wine, such as Sauvignon Blanc
3¼ cups vegetable broth
1 cup fresh shelled or frozen peas
Salt to taste
Freshly ground black pepper to taste

DIRECTIONS

Cut the green ramp leaves off the stems, and chop the stems. Bring a pot of water to boil. Drop in the ramp leaves and blanch for about one minute. Drain and purée in a food processor with the lemon zest, juice from 1 lemon, parsley and 2½ tablespoons olive oil. Set aside until needed.

For the halved lemon, squeeze the juice into a large bowl of cold water, and throw the squeezed lemon halves into the water, too.

Peel away the tough outer leaves of the baby artichokes, until just the more tender light green leaves are left. Cut off the top ½ inch from the artichoke and trim the stem of any tough-looking parts. Quarter the artichokes and put them in the lemon water while you start the risotto.

Heat 1½ tablespoons olive oil over medium heat in a large heavy saucepan. Drain the artichokes from the lemon water and sauté them for 5 minutes. Add the garlic and chopped ramp stems and cook 5 minutes more. Add the quinoa and sauté for 1 minute, stirring constantly. Add the wine and fresh thyme, and cook until the liquid is absorbed, about 1 minute.

Add the broth; bring to a boil, lower heat and simmer 10 minutes, stirring frequently. Add the peas and simmer another 4–6 minutes, stirring often. (The quinoa should be almost soft but still have a bit of a crunch. You should see a little white ring separating from each grain.) Season with salt and pepper to taste. Stir in ramp purée and serve.

RECIPE AND PHOTO BY **CATHY ELTON**, *WHAT WOULD CATHY EAT?* BLOG
(WWW.WHATWOULDCATHYEAT.COM)

SPRING VEGETABLE CURRY WITH RAMP CILANTRO CHUTNEY

This vegetarian curry is made with special ingredients that are available here in upstate NY in the spring: ramps, wild fiddleheads and dandelion greens. Both recipes were inspired by the talented Monica Bhide's wonderful book, Modern Spice: Inspired Indian Flavors for the Contemporary Kitchen.

Serves 2–3

❧ INGREDIENTS

2 tablespoons organic coconut oil or ghee
1 teaspoon black mustard seeds
1½-inch piece fresh ginger, peeled and minced
4 whole ramps, chopped fine (or substitute 4 cloves
    peeled garlic instead)
1 Serrano chili pepper, minced (for spicy curry, leave seeds in)
1 large sweet potato, peeled and chopped into cubes
1 can (14-ounce) organic whole coconut milk
1 cup fiddleheads, rinsed very well and cleaned of all debris
    (or substitute 1 cup asparagus tips)
1 cup chopped dandelion greens (or substitute collards or kale)
1 bell pepper, cored, seeded and chopped
    (I used half of a red one and half of an orange one)
1 large tomato, chopped
1 teaspoon turmeric
½ teaspoon ground coriander
¼ teaspoon sea salt, optional

⟋⟍ DIRECTIONS

In a large skillet or wok, melt the coconut oil or ghee over medium heat. Add the mustard seeds and cook for a minute or two until they "pop," then add the ginger, minced ramps, and chili pepper. Stir everything around for a minute or so.

Add the chopped sweet potato to the pan along with the coconut milk. Bring to a boil, then reduce heat to a simmer. Cook for about 15 minutes, stirring occasionally. Add a little water if the liquid seems too thick.

While the sweet potato is cooking, place your clean fiddleheads in a pot of water and bring to a boil. Allow to boil for 10 minutes (fiddleheads are a wild food, and this is the recommended preparation so that you don't become ill from them…better safe than sorry). After boiling for 10 minutes, drain and set aside.

Add the fiddleheads, dandelion greens, bell pepper and tomato to the sweet potatoes. Simmer for another 15 minutes, or until vegetables are very tender, again adding a little water if necessary.

Mix in the spices (and salt, if using). Cook for another minute or two. Taste and adjust the spices, if necessary. Remove from heat and allow to cool slightly while you proceed with the chutney.

RAMP CILANTRO CHUTNEY

Yields about 1 cup

❧ INGREDIENTS

¾ cup (approximately) fresh cilantro, chopped
Green tops of 4 ramps, chopped fine
   (use ¼ cup chopped mint if you don't have ramps)
Juice of ½ fresh lime
1 teaspoon organic sugar

❧ DIRECTIONS

Mix minced ramp tops with cilantro in a small bowl. Add lime juice and sugar. Mix well, and serve over the curry.

RECIPES AND PHOTOS BY **WINNIE ABRAMSON**, *HEALTHY GREEN KITCHEN* BLOG
(WWW.HEALTHYGREENKITCHEN.COM)

Salads
& Soups

RAMP GREEN GODDESS DRESSING

I have used this as a dressing for baby spinach salad topped with roasted shiitake mushrooms, and as a sauce over baked wild salmon. It would complement roasted or grilled spring lamb and roasted asparagus. Also great tossed with boiled new potatoes for a zingy potato salad.

Yields about 2¼ cups

INGREDIENTS

1 cup high quality mayonnaise, plus ¼ cup lemon juice
(or 1 cup homemade lemon mayo)
1 cup sour cream
¼ cup young ramp greens, washed well and coarsely chopped
¼ cup parsley, coarsely chopped
2 teaspoons arugula, finely chopped
1 tablespoon white wine or white balsamic vinegar
½ teaspoon kosher or sea salt
½ teaspoon freshly ground black pepper

Optional:
1 teaspoon anchovy paste or ¼ teaspoon fish sauce
1 teaspoon chopped garlic

DIRECTIONS

Combine all ingredients in a food processor or blender. Purée until smooth, you can run a little longer to be sure you get a very creamy texture. Use immediately or chill until ready to serve. This recipe will increase in intensity of ramp flavor over days. If you plan to make this ahead by a day or two, definitely refrain from using the garlic, unless you know your guests love garlic.

RECIPE AND PHOTO BY **BARBARA PRICE**, *GREENWICH MEAL TIME* BLOG
(WWW.BARBARAPRICE.WORDPRESS.COM)

RAMP RANCH DRESSING

Perfect for salads, but it's also a terrific dressing for crab cakes!

Yields 1 cup

❧ INGREDIENTS

½ cup sour cream or low fat yogurt
   (I like vanilla – makes it a bit sweet against the ramps)
½ cup mayonnaise
1 teaspoon lemon juice
1 clove garlic, pressed
½ teaspoon whole grain mustard
1 small bunch ramps, washed and chopped
2 tablespoons finely chopped parsley
1 tablespoon chopped fresh dill, or ¼ teaspoon dry
Salt and pepper to taste

❧ DIRECTIONS

In a medium bowl stir together sour cream and mayonnaise until fully incorporated. Add the rest of the ingredients until mixed well, adjust salt and pepper to taste.

RECIPE AND PHOTO BY **CHEF TODD C. GRAY**,
EQUINOX AND WATERSHED RESTAURANTS, WASHINGTON, D.C.

SHAVED ASPARAGUS & RAMP SALAD
WITH PARMESAN & LEMON VINAIGRETTE

I was out fishing one day and found myself in the middle of a field full of ramps. I had my knife and a plastic bag so I dug up about 5 pounds of ramps with leaves attached. Back home, I prepared them several ways — candied, pickled, in omelets — and I still had a big bag left. I had gotten some asparagus from a buddy of mine that were about the size of those small bats they give away at baseball games, but sweet and tender. Perfect for an asparagus and ramp salad. Not only did it turn out to be a great salad, but it also made a great topping for bratwurst.

Serves 6 (½ cup each)

INGREDIENTS

1 pound shaved asparagus
½ pound ramp leaves, cut about ½-inch thick

DIRECTIONS

Toss together in a bowl and dress with lemon vinaigrette.

VINAIGRETTE

¼ cup fresh lemon juice
½ cup olive oil
½ cup Parmesan cheese, shaved
Salt and pepper to taste

Whisk together the olive oil and lemon juice, then add Parmesan and season to taste with salt and pepper.

RECIPE AND PHOTO BY **JAMIE CARLSON**, *YOU HAVE TO COOK IT RIGHT* BLOG
(HTTP://YOUHAVETOCOOKITRIGHT.BLOGSPOT.COM)

DANDELION GREENS SALAD WITH RAMPS, BACON & BLUE CHEESE

There is nothing bashful about this salad. It features lots of assertive flavors.

Serves 1–2

INGREDIENTS

Salad Ingredients
3 strips bacon, preferably pastured and preservative-free*
8 ramps, bottom white parts only
4 cups chopped organic dandelion greens
   (if unavailable, use your favorite greens)
1 cup chopped organic parsley
Approximately 3 tablespoons blue cheese
   (I use Cashel Blue Irish Farmhouse cheese)

DRESSING

Juice from ½ fresh lemon, preferably a Meyer lemon
¼ cup best olive oil
½ teaspoon Dijon mustard
2 ramps, bottom white parts only, minced
Pinch sea salt

DIRECTIONS

For the salad: If using bacon, cook it in a hot skillet until crisp on both sides. Remove to a towel to drain and cool. Leave the hot bacon fat in the pan over medium heat.

Toss the ramps into the hot bacon fat (or use an equal amount of hot olive oil). Allow ramps to cook for a minute or two, until nicely browned on all sides. Remove and allow to cool.

Crumble the bacon into a small bowl and set aside.

Coarsely chop the cooked ramps and mix in a medium bowl with the greens, parsley, and crumbled bacon. Set aside while you make the dressing.

For the dressing: Mix all dressing ingredients in a small bowl and pour over the salad.

Crumble blue cheese over the salad and serve.

* If you don't want to use bacon, you can sizzle your ramps in some olive oil instead.

RECIPE AND PHOTO BY **WINNIE ABRAMSON**, *HEALTHY GREEN KITCHEN* BLOG
(WWW.HEALTHYGREENKITCHEN.COM)

CHICKPEA & SPRING GREEN SALAD WITH LEMONY VINAIGRETTE

This salad goes nicely with a crisp Sauvingnon Blanc and some crusty artisan bread.

Serves 4 as a main course, 6 as a side

➤ INGREDIENTS

3 cups cooked garbanzo beans (chickpeas),
   or 2 (15-ounce) cans, drained and rinsed
6 cups (about 5 ounces) loosely packed baby spinach leaves,
   washed and spun dry
1 bunch small ramps (about a dozen), washed well and
   thinly sliced – bulbs and greens included
6 medium radishes, scrubbed and thinly sliced
2 ounces semi-hard cheese, grated, such as
   Sprout Creek Bogart, Asiago or Pecorino

➤ VINAIGRETTE

Zest and juice from one small lemon
5–6 tablespoons extra-virgin olive oil
1 tablespoon white wine vinegar
½ teaspoon salt
½ teaspoon freshly ground black pepper

➤ DIRECTIONS

In a large bowl combine chickpeas, spinach, ramps and radishes. Toss to mix.In a small bowl, combine lemon zest and juice, vinegar, olive oil, salt and pepper. Whisk well to combine and emulsify the oil. Taste and adjust seasonings if necessary.

Drizzle vinaigrette over salad, tossing as you go. Stop adding when most of the spinach leaves are coated, but there is no dressing gathering at the bottom of the bowl. Toss well and allow the spinach leaves to wilt slightly. Add grated cheese and toss again. Cheese should dissolve into the dressing somewhat, making the dressing richer but without adding an overall cheese flavor. Taste and adjust amounts of vinaigrette, cheese, salt or pepper. Serve immediately. (Best fresh, but if you must, store the salad components and vinaigrette separately, and combine just before serving.)

VEGAN OPTION
The cheese acts to tone down the lemony tartness of the vinaigrette. For a vegan version, a small amount of soy yogurt added to the vinaigrette may do the trick.

RECIPE AND PHOTO BY **KAELA PORTER**, *LOCAL KITCHEN* BLOG
(WWW.LOCALKITCHENBLOG.COM)

CREMA OF RAMPS WITH WILD ASPARAGUS

Serves 8

⚘ INGREDIENTS

2 teaspoons oil or butter
2 cups diced red or Yukon gold potatoes
2 stalks celery, finely diced
8–10 whole ramps, whites separated from greens, reserved
½ large sweet onion or 1 whole leek (white and part of green)
32 ounces (4 cups) chicken stock or homemade vegetable stock
2 cups asparagus pieces
1 teaspoon salt
Pepper to taste

⚘ DIRECTIONS

Start with a large stockpot, warming the oil or butter. Dice potatoes into 1-inch cubes, small enough to cook fast. I leave the skins on because I'm going to purée the whole thing and the dark flecks don't bother me. Or peel potatoes before dicing.

Add diced potatoes, celery, ramp whites, onion, and/or leeks to the stockpot and stir to coat with the fat. Sauté for 2 minutes, then add ½ cup stock and cover with a tight fitting lid. Allow to braise for about 10 minutes, until vegetable are tender. Add remaining broth and bring to a simmer. Add the stems of asparagus to the soup pot now, reserving the tips for the final step.

When the potatoes are completely cooked through and tender, remove the pot from the heat. Stir in the coarsely chopped ramp greens.

To purée: I use a blender, but an immersion wand can work fine, though the result is not as elegant. In a blender, work in two batches, puréeing until the soup is very smooth. This will yield a creamy soup flecked with bright green ramps and tiny bits of red potato skins. For a very refined presentation you can strain the soup through a sieve to remove any larger particles, yielding a pure green, velvety-textured soup.

To finish: Return the pureed soup to the pot and warm before serving. Toss in asparagus tips, remove from heat and allow to sit for 1 minute. Add salt and pepper to taste. Serve hot with a garnish of crisp bacon, a swirl of crème fraîche or a sprinkling of chives.

RECIPE AND PHOTO BY **BARBARA PRICE**, *GREENWICH MEAL TIME* BLOG
(WWW.BARBARAPRICE.WORDPRESS.COM)

EASY MIXED BEAN & RAMP SOUP

Serves 6 adults easily, with room for seconds

🍂 INGREDIENTS

1 jar Randall Deluxe Mixed Beans (48-ounce)*
½ pound sliced bacon (thick-sliced peppered bacon is best)
1 large can (48-ounce) chicken broth (48-ounce),
    or use chicken bouillon
2 large (peeled) Idaho potatoes
1 large bunch ramps
Salt and pepper to taste

🍂 DIRECTIONS

In a large pot (with a lid), combine undrained mixed beans and chicken broth. Cover and simmer on low heat. Slice raw bacon into 1-inch squares and add to pot. Dice potatoes into medium sized cubes and add to pot.

Wash and clean ramps, removing only roots. Dice fresh ramps into 1-inch pieces using white stem and lower half portion of green leaf (non-bitter). For young ramps, use entire stem and leaf, minus the root. Add to pot and slow cook on low heat until potatoes are tender (but with a nice firm texture), stirring occasionally to prevent sticking. Approximate time is one hour. I told you that was easy!

Note: You can go old-school and boil a chicken for the broth and make your own mixed beans from scratch. If you must thin out the soup while cooking, avoid adding water and use only broth. If you have company, simply double the recipe.

A word about ramps: It has been suggested that the Native American Indians used to leave or return the root caps from the harvested ramps to insure future crops. I support this wisdom and encourage others to do the same.

If you are not sure about Randall Mixed Beans you can find them on the Internet.

RECIPE AND PHOTOS BY **GHOST**, NORTHERN MICHIGAN

RAMP UDON SOUP WITH BACON CONSOMMÉ & ASPARAGUS TEMPURA

If you plan ahead for this unusual ramp soup you can pull it together very quickly at the last minute. The bacon consommé should be started at least a week in advance. The tempura batter can be made ½ hour in advance, and you can even sauté the ramps ahead of time. If making homemade udon from scratch, you will need 3-3½ hours advance prep time.

Serves 6–8

INGREDIENTS

Bacon consommé (recipe below)
Udon (homemade preferred – see recipe on our blog,
   Habeas Brûlee – but store-bought will do)
Asparagus tempura – 2 stalks per serving/person (recipe below)
Ramps (8 or so leaves and bulbs per person/serving)
Safflower oil (or peanut or corn oil)
Salt and freshly ground black pepper, to taste

BACON CONSOMMÉ (made well ahead)

1 pound bacon
3 quarts or so of water
Gelatin (¼ ounce per quart of water)

DIRECTIONS

In a large pot, fry the bacon until delicious. Add the water and simmer for an hour or so. If the flavor isn't sufficiently infused at that point, blend the bacon and water together.

Strain through a fine mesh strainer. Reduce the resulting liquid to taste.

Measure the weight of the liquid you end up with, and measure out .7% gelatin by weight (or one ¼-ounce packet Knox gelatin per quart). Take a cup of the liquid and set it aside to cool a bit, then stir in the gelatin. Stir back into the rest of the liquid.

Put the liquid in a plastic zipper bag and freeze. Once frozen, remove from freezer and transfer it to your fridge with a cheesecloth-lined strainer set over a bowl. As the block melts, bacon consommé will drip through the cheesecloth into the bowl below. The gelatin that remains acts as a strainer so that the dripping liquid is perfectly clear.

Consommé can be frozen until needed.

ASPARAGUS TEMPURA BATTER

½ cup ice water
½ cup vodka
1⅛ cup all-purpose flour
⅛ teaspoon baking soda
½ teaspoon salt, or to taste

DIRECTIONS

Stir batter ingredients together with a fork. Don't spend too long on this, and leave batter slightly lumpy. Allow to chill in the fridge, at least ½ hour or so.

Clean the ramps and cut off and discard the root ends. Cut each ramp into three sections by first cutting the leaves from the stems/bulbs, then cutting the stems/bulbs in half.

Sauté ramps in a bit of safflower oil, adding salt and pepper to taste. Set aside.

Prepare the udon noodles. If using store-bought, bring large pot of water to a boil and follow package directions. For homemade, follow instructions on our blog.

For the tempura: Clean and dry asparagus, cutting off woody ends. (I like to snap them off, then trim the ragged ends for serving.)

Heat up enough oil for deep-frying to 425°F. Dip asparagus in the tempura batter, one stalk at a time. With your fingers, scrape off any excess batter, leaving the asparagus only lightly covered. Fry just a few stalks at a time, not allowing the oil to go below 375°F.

Deep-fry the asparagus until golden brown. This should happen very quickly, so don't walk away! Then remove the tempura with a slotted spoon and set it on a rack or paper towel-covered plate to drain. Wait for the oil to come back up to 425°F before adding in the next batch each time. Serve immediately.

To serve: Drop udon into each bowl and mix in ramps. Pour in bacon consommé, and garnish bowl with asparagus tempura.

RECIPE BY **DAVID TURNER** AND **DANIELLE SUCHER**.
JACK RESTAURANT, NEW YORK CITY. *HABEAS BRÛLEE* BLOG.
(WWW.HABEASBRULEE.COM)
PHOTO BY **DANIELLE SUCHER**

THE L TRAIN RAMP SOUP

On a Sunday in May, the Brooklyn-based culinary event group a razor, a shiny knife *(actual name) created a surprise pop-up restaurant on the L Train, serving a six-course luncheon for 12 as it traveled between 8th Avenue and Canarsie Station. This ramp soup was the third course. The subway luncheon was accompanied by readings from* The Great Gatsby.

This elegant gluten-free dish is an assemblage of ramp soup, black garlic purée, ham tuile, confit cippolini onions and morels, and dehydrated ramp leaves.

Serves 4

❧ RAMP SOUP

1¼ cup stock
1½ ounces ramp tops (leaves)
1 teaspoon olive oil
½ cup sweet onion, diced
3½ tablespoons diced ramp bottoms
3½ tablespoons diced celery
3½ tablespoons diced leeks
Pinch of salt, and to taste
4 teaspoons cream
White pepper to taste

8 dehydrated ramp tops, for garnish

❧ DIRECTIONS

In a saucepan, bring stock to a boil and blanch ramp tops for several seconds, then shock in an ice bath. Reserve.

In a second saucepan, heat olive oil, then add diced onions, ramp bottoms, celery and leeks, and a pinch of salt. Sauté on medium-low heat until vegetables are softened but not too colored, then add stock and cook until reduced by one-third. Add cream, bring heat to low-simmer and let cook for 8 minutes.

Remove from heat and place in blender. Add ramp tops and blend on high for 5 minutes. Pass through a chinois (fine mesh strainer), season to taste and reserve.

BLACK GARLIC PURÉE

1 ounce black garlic, peeled
4 teaspoons extra virgin olive oil
1 teaspoon mandioca flour (gluten-free,
   found in Latin America markets)

DIRECTIONS

Place all ingredients into a food processor and process until smooth. Add to a squirt bottle and reserve warm until service.

HAM TUILE

8 slices Prosciutto di Parma or equivalent cured ham

DIRECTIONS

Heat oven to 275°F. Place ham slices between 2 pieces of parchment paper and press between 2 sheet trays. Place in oven until crisp. Remove and store in an airtight container.

CONFIT CIPPOLINI ONONS AND MORELS

1 pound duck fat
8 cippolini onions, cleaned, trimmed top and bottom,
  and peeled
8 morels, washed

Place duck fat into a small pot and heat until liquid. Place onions and morels into duck fat and cook over low heat until tender. Reserve until service, keeping onions and morels covered in fat so they are not exposed to the air. At service, reheat thoroughly and hold over heat.

PRESENTATION

Bowls should be flat and wide, warmed before service.

Squirt a dollop of black garlic purée just off-center of the bowl. Place one confit onion and one morel in the bowl, opposite the garlic purée. Place a ham tuile on the edge of the bowl. Put a dehydrated ramp top between the garlic purée and the confit onion and morel, so the top hangs over the ham off the side of the bowl.

Pour soup (warm, from a silver teapot) along the outer edge of the bowl until onion, morel and purée are submerged. Offer peppermill to taste, tableside.

RECIPE BY **A RAZOR, A SHINY KNIFE**, WITH **LINDA LOU**
(WWW.ARAZORASHINYKNIFE.COM)
PHOTOS BY **STEPH GORALNICK**

Ramps & Eggs

BUCKWHEAT CRÊPES WITH EGG, RAMPS & BACON

(a dairy-free recipe)

Makes 8 crêpes

❧ BATTER

¾ cup plus 1 tablespoon buckwheat flour
⅓ cup all-purpose flour
½ teaspoon salt
1 tablespoon margarine, melted
½ teaspoon toasted sesame oil
1½ cups soymilk
3 eggs

❧ FILLING

8 eggs
4 slices thick-cut bacon
1 tablespoon olive oil
12–14 ramps (6 ounces)
Salt and pepper to taste
Oil or margarine for coating the pan

❧ DIRECTIONS

First, make the batter: In a medium bowl sift together the dry ingredients. In a separate bowl mix together the wet ingredients. Add the wet ingredients to the dry and beat until smooth. Cover and chill the batter for 30 minutes.

Turn on broiler and place oven rack in the top position. Lay out a sheet pan or cookie sheet.

For the filling: Chop bacon and cook until crispy. Drain and set aside. Wash and slice the ramps, keeping the green tops separate from the white bottoms. Cook ramp bottoms in a pan with the olive oil over medium-low heat. When the bottoms are softened add the green tops and toss. Remove pan from heat and season with salt and pepper to taste.

To make a crêpe: Heat a non-stick skillet or crêpe pan over medium-high heat. When the pan is hot coat the inside with oil or margarine. Pour in ¼ cup of crêpe batter and immediately swirl to coat the pan evenly. Cook until the edges dry out and the top is mostly set. Loosen the crêpe around the edges with a spatula and then flip.

As soon as it is flipped, add ⅛ of the cooked ramps to the middle of the crêpe and crack an egg on top. Sprinkle on ⅛ of the bacon and flip up the sides of the crêpe to form a rough square with the egg exposed in the center. Slide the filled crêpe out of the pan and onto the sheet pan. Repeat 7 more times.

Place the sheet pan with under the broiler and cook until egg whites are set (30 seconds to 1 minute). Plate with salt and freshly ground black pepper on top.

RECIPE AND PHOTO BY **MAGGIE RAPTIS**, *DOG HILL KITCHEN* BLOG
(WWW.DOGHILLKITCHEN.COM)

EGGS WITH RAMPS & BACON

Serves 1–2

INGREDIENTS

¼ pound slab bacon, cut into lardons (1-inch by ¼-inch by ¼-inch)
½ cup water
2 tablespoons butter
16 ramps, washed and ends trimmed
Kosher salt and freshly ground black pepper, to taste
2–4 large eggs
Red chili flakes

DIRECTIONS

Place bacon in a 10-inch nonstick skillet and add water. Bring to a simmer over high heat and cook, stirring occasionally, until water has evaporated and bacon is well-rendered and crisp, about 15 minutes. Transfer bacon to a small bowl, but leave rendered fat in skillet.

Add butter to bacon fat in skillet and heat over high heat until foaming has subsided and butter begins to brown. Add ramps and cook, stirring and tossing occasionally until well browned. Season to taste with salt and pepper. Transfer ramps to bowl with bacon.

Crack eggs directly into same skillet and fry over medium-high heat until whites are set on top and brown and crisp on the bottom, and yolk is still runny, about 2 minutes. Transfer eggs to a plate, pour any remaining bacon fat and butter from the skillet over them, season to taste with salt, pepper and chili flakes, and serve with bacon and ramps.

RECIPE AND PHOTO BY **J. KENJI LOPEZ-ALT**, *SERIOUS EATS* BLOG
(WWW.SERIOUSEATS.COM)

RISOTTO CAKE WITH CRISPY RAMPS (AND A FRIED EGG)

Vegetarian and gluten-free; not vegan

This could be a hangover breakfast, though I'd serve it anytime. Whenever I make risotto, I make extra so that I can have risotto cakes the next day. If you don't have leftover risotto, you could do this dish with grilled toast (brioche, ideally), or even a savory French toast.

Serves 1

INGREDIENTS

6 ramps, white parts only, trimmed and halved lengthwise
3 tablespoons butter
½ cup leftover risotto (any kind without too many mix-ins)
1 egg
Salt, to taste
A few oregano leaves
Aged balsamic vinegar

DIRECTIONS

Melt butter in a frying pan over medium-high heat. Fry the ramps, keeping the temperature just below where the butter will burn. Cook until well browned. Season with salt. Remove ramps, leaving the butter behind.

Form the risotto into about a 3½-inch wide patty, ½-inch thick. If it won't hold together, mix in a beaten egg. Use a ring mold to form it more neatly if you like. In the same frying pan, cook the risotto cake on both sides until deep golden brown. Remove to a warmed plate and season with salt.

In the same pan, adding a little more butter if needed, fry the egg until the white is done and the yolk is still liquid.* Again if you like, you can use a well oiled ring mold to hold the egg's shape. It is helpful to add a little water and cover the pan to get the top of the whites to cook.

To serve, put the egg on top of the risotto cake, and the ramps on top of the egg. Garnish with oregano leaves and a drizzle of well-aged balsamic vinegar.

Use your own judgment about the risks of eating undercooked eggs.

RECIPE AND PHOTO BY **MICHAEL NATKIN**, *HERBIVORACIOUS* BLOG
(WWW.HERBIVORACIOUS.COM)

RAMPS, MORELS & FRESH PEAS WITH POACHED EGGS

This is a simple but wonderfully comforting and delicious dish that works for breakfast, lunch or dinner. The fresh morels add a richness to the dish that works so well with the garlicky punch of the ramps, but any fresh wild mushroom would also work well.

Serves 2

❧ INGREDIENTS

2 Yukon Gold potatoes, cut into ½-inch cubes
Salt for the pot
¼ cup fresh peas, removed from pod
2 tablespoons butter
1 tablespoon olive oil
3–4 ounces fresh morel mushrooms, cut in half lengthwise
Salt and fresh black pepper to taste
10–12 fresh ramps, cleaned and cut into diagonal strips
2 slices good toast (I prefer sourdough)
4 farm fresh eggs
Shaved Pecorino Romano cheese to taste

❧ DIRECTIONS

Bring a large pot of water to a boil. Season well with salt and blanch the potatoes for about 5 minutes or until they are cooked to al dente. Remove the potatoes with a slotted spoon and set aside. In the same boiling water, blanch the peas for 1–2 minutes. Remove and set aside.

Prepare a pot for poaching the eggs by bringing at least two inches of water to a boil, then reducing heat to low. Keep on low until you are ready to poach the eggs.

In a saucepan, heat the butter and oil over medium heat. Add the potatoes and mushrooms, season with salt and pepper, and let caramelize for about 5 minutes. Add the ramps and sauté for another two minutes, tossing or stirring frequently. Add the peas and remove the pan from the heat.

In the last 5 minutes, put your bread in the toaster and poach your eggs.

To assemble: Place the toast on the dish and top with the sautéed vegetables. Add two poached eggs, garnish with the shaving of Pecorino Romano cheese, crack fresh black pepper over the dish and serve immediately.

RECIPE AND PHOTO BY **AIMEE MOTT**, *THE FRESH DISH* BLOG
(WWW.THEFRESHDISH.COM)

SPRING VEGETABLE FRITTATA

This year we tried ramps two different ways. We pickled the stems, and with the leaves we made this delicious spring vegetable frittata.

Serves 6

INGREDIENTS

Olive oil, for the baking dish
10 small morels (or 5 large ones), sliced into thin strips
2 plum tomatoes, diced
1 cup ramp leaves, loosely packed, julienned
1 cup baby spinach, loosely packed, julienned
4 stalks asparagus, cleaned and cut into 1-inch pieces
6 eggs
Salt and pepper, to taste
1 cup shredded part-skim mozzarella (more or less, to taste)

DIRECTIONS

Preheat oven to 350°F. Lightly oil a 1½-quart baking dish.

Arrange morels, tomatoes, ramps, spinach and asparagus in the baking dish.

Crack the eggs into a bowl, add salt and pepper and beat until incorporated. Carefully pour over vegetables in the baking dish.

Bake for approximately 20 minutes. Check around the 18-minute mark to make sure the eggs are not cooking too quickly. Do not overcook. (The eggs should have body but still look wet and glossy.)

Remove from the oven and turn on your broiler. Sprinkle mozzarella over top of frittata and return to the oven until the cheese melts and starts to bubble and turn golden.

RECIPE AND PHOTO BY **ADELINE CHENG**, *MY KIND OF FOOD* BLOG
(HTTP://MYKINDOFFOOD.BLOGSPOT.COM)

Biscuits & Muffins, Etc.

RAMP PESTO CORNMEAL MUFFINS

These savory muffins have just the right amount of pesto flavor – not too overpowering, but enough to enliven your taste buds. If you don't have ramps, use any pesto you like in this recipe.

Yields 12 muffins

PESTO

1 bunch ramps, white bulb and green leafy parts, chopped
1 cup cilantro
⅓ cup mint leaves
⅓ cup walnuts
½ cup grated high-quality Parmesan cheese (not the Kraft stuff)
Juice of ½ lemon
Salt, to taste
⅓ cup extra-virgin olive oil

DIRECTIONS

Place ramps, cilantro, mint and walnuts in the bowl of a food processor and pulse a few times until coarsely minced. Add cheese, lemon juice and salt, and process until combined. Scrape the sides of the bowl. Through the feed tube, add olive oil while machine is running and process until slightly grainy.

🍃 MUFFINS

1 cup cornmeal
1 cup whole wheat
   pastry flour
2 teaspoons baking
powder
1 tablespoon sugar
½ teaspoon salt
1 egg
½ cup milk
½ cup plain yogurt
⅓ cup oil
3 tablespoons ramp pesto

🍃 DIRECTIONS

Preheat oven to 350°F.

In a bowl, mix together cornmeal, flour, baking powder, sugar and salt.

In a separate bowl, whisk together egg, milk, yogurt, oil and 3 tablespoons pesto, until everything is combined and smooth. Stir wet ingredients into dry ingredients.

Divide mixture among 12 muffin cups. Bake for 15 minutes, or until a tester comes out clean. Let cool 5 minutes before unmolding.

RECIPE AND PHOTO BY **MATTHEW KADEY**, *MUFFIN TIN MANIA* BLOG
(WWW.MUFFINTINMANIA.COM)

BUTTERMILK RAMP BISCUITS (1)

Makes 12–16 biscuits

◈ INGREDIENTS

¼ pound smoked hog jowl, cut into ¼-inch dice
  (or substitute thick sliced bacon)
4 cups all-purpose flour
2 tablespoons baking powder
1 tablespoon baking soda
1 teaspoon salt
½ cup pure lard or shortening
1 cup thinly sliced fresh ramps, including greens
  (reserve 1 tablespoon white portion for ramp butter)
2 cups buttermilk, as needed
¼ pound softened butter
Pinch paprika

◈ DIRECTIONS

Preheat oven to 425°F.

Cook diced hog jowl or bacon in a large skillet over medium-high heat until crisp. Remove from pan and drain on paper towels until cool.

Sift flour, baking powder and baking soda and salt together into a large bowl. Using a pastry cutter or two knives, "cut in" the lard or shortening until it's in little flour-coated pieces the size of a grain of rice. Take care that you do not cut it too finely. It's these tiny fat globules that make biscuits light and flaky.

Add sliced ramps and crisped jowl. Gently stir in just enough buttermilk so dry ingredients form a soft ball of dough. Do not

mix more than absolutely necessary. Don't worry if there are still lumps in the dough.

Turn dough out onto a well-floured surface. Dust your hands with flour and gently fold dough on itself just until ingredients are evenly incorporated. Be careful not to overwork dough. With a rolling pin well-dusted with flour, roll out dough to about ¾-inch thick. Cut biscuits with a sharp biscuit cutter or 3-inch diameter tin can with both ends cut out. Do not use a glass or jar. You need a sharp, clean cut to get high, flaky biscuits. Gently knead leftover dough back together into a mass and roll out again to cut remaining biscuits.

Arrange biscuits about 2 inches apart on a lightly greased baking sheet.

For the ramp butter: Lightly cook the reserved 1 tablespoon of ramps in a little of the fat from the hog jowls until slightly softened and translucent. Set aside to cool. Place softened butter in a small bowl and mix in the ramps and paprika, stirring vigorously until butter is smooth and all ingredients are incorporated. Or use a small food processor.

Brush tops of biscuits with some of the ramp-infused butter and bake for 15–20 minutes, or until golden brown. Serve immediately with remaining ramp butter.

RECIPE AND PHOTO BY **DAVID EGER**, *EARTHY DELIGHTS* BLOG
(WWW.EARTHYDELIGHTSBLOG.COM)

BUTTERMILK RAMP BISCUITS (2)

Yields about 24 biscuits

INGREDIENTS

2 cups ramps, bulbs and leaves, cleaned and sliced
1½ cups buttermilk
2 tablespoons heavy cream
3½ cups all-purpose flour
1 teaspoon baking powder
1½ tablespoons baking soda
1 tablespoon salt
2 teaspoons coriander seeds, crushed
6 ounces butter, cold and cubed
¼ cup grated Pecorino cheese, optional

DIRECTIONS

Preheat oven to 425°F. Combine buttermilk, cream and ramps and soak for up to an hour – this will allow the ramps to steep into the buttermilk and intensify their rampiness.

In a food processor or standing mixer combine flour, baking powder, salt and 1 teaspoon coriander seeds.

Cut the cold butter into the dry ingredients with a few pulses until the mixture is mealy but still a bit chunky. Add the buttermilk mixture and combine just until the dough comes together.

Turn out onto a floured surface and roll to about ½-inch thick. The dough might be tacky – dust with more flour to keep it from sticking as you roll. Cut out circles with a cookie cutter, or use a knife for a more rustic look.

Place onto a lined baking sheet, brush with heavy cream and top with crushed coriander and shredded cheese. Bake for 16–20 minutes, until the biscuits are risen and golden brown on top.

RECIPE AND PHOTO BY **ARCHANA RAO** OF LOVE STREET CAKES
AND *DON'T F WITH CHEF* BLOG
(HTTP://DONTFWITHCHEF.BLOGSPOT.COM)

RAMP FRITTERS

FRITTER BATTER (from Richard Olney's *Simple French Food*)
¾ cup flour
2 eggs, separated with whites set aside
¾ cup beer (I like Bass pale ale)
2 tablespoons olive oil
¼ teaspoon salt

FRITTER MIXTURE

2 zucchinis, peeled and grated
15 small to medium ramps, cleaned (treatment below)
1 stem of wild garlic or a small garlic clove, finely minced
Juice of ½ lemon
Splash of olive oil, plus some for the pan
Salt and pepper, to taste
2 tablespoons finely chopped parsley

First, create the base of the batter by combining the flour, egg yolks, beer, olive oil and salt in a bowl and whisk just enough to blend everything together smoothly. Let it rest for at least an hour, which according to Olney helps it better coat the items to be fried (*this can be skipped, given this recipe's particular approach, but I did it anyway*).

In a colander, thoroughly squeeze the moisture out of the grated zucchini with your hands. Place in a bowl. Finely chop the stems of the ramps and chop a fine chiffonade of the leaves. Add both to the bowl. Stir in the garlic, lemon juice, olive oil and a pinch of salt and pepper. Let this rest as well while the batter sits.

Beat the egg whites until the peaks hold, and fold them into the batter. Gently stir the vegetables into the batter.

Heat up some olive oil (or a mixture of olive oil and vegetable/canola oil) in a large cast iron pan on medium-high heat, enough to well-coat the surface of the pan. When a drop of water jumps and sizzles in the pan, you are ready. With a decent-size soup-spoon, place spoonfuls of batter around the pan, being careful not to overcrowd or let fritters touch each other. Cook until golden brown on both sides, then remove to a drying rack or a plate with paper towel.

Serve with some fresh lemon juice and taste for salt and pepper. I also suspect that crème fraîche in addition to the lemon would make a wonderful complement to the fritters.

RECIPE BY **GIFF CONSTABLE**, *CONSTABLE'S LARDER* BLOG
(WWW.CONSTABLESLARDER.COM)

SWEET CORN GRIDDLE CAKES

Serves 2 as an entrée and 4 as appetizers

~ INGREDIENTS

1 cup vegetable stock
¾ cup freeze dried corn
¼ cup cornmeal
1 cup buttermilk
2 eggs
⅔ cup all-purpose flour
3 teaspoons baking powder
1 teaspoon salt
¼ teaspoon baking soda
¼ cup melted butter
Vegetable oil, or clarified butter, as needed

~ DIRECTIONS

Bring vegetable stock to a boil and add ¼ cup freeze dried corn. Allow to rehydrate for 10 minutes. Meanwhile, grind the cornmeal and freeze dried corn into a fine powder in a blender or spice grinder. Remove corn from vegetable stock and set aside. Pour the stock over the corn powder and stir to rehydrate. Whisk in the buttermilk and eggs.

Combine the dry ingredients and whisk into the corn mixture. Drizzle in the melted butter and stir to incorporate. Finally, fold in the rehydrated corn kernels.

Heat oil or clarified butter in a cast iron pan over high heat and use a 1-ounce ladle to form corn cakes. Cook for 1 minute, flip, then cook for 30 seconds longer.

🌿 SAUTÉED RAMPS

1 pound ramps, rinsed
4 ounces clarified butter
1 shallot, finely minced
½ ounce sherry wine
Juice of 1 lemon
Salt and pepper to taste

Separate ramp whites from the greens. Slice any large whites in half. In a sauté pan heat 2 ounces butter and add ramp whites and shallot. Cook for about 2 minutes, or until slightly browned and softened. Deglaze with sherry wine and season to taste. Heat the remaining butter in a separate sauté pan. Add the greens and toss lightly. Add lemon juice and cook until almost completely wilted. Remove from the heat.

To assemble and serve:

½ cup sour cream

Place three corn cakes on the plate, followed by a portion of wilted ramp leaves, then sautéed ramp whites. Finish with a drizzling of sour cream. Enjoy.

RECIPE BY **GARRETT KERN**, *GARRETT'S TABLE* BLOG. PHOTO BY **JUSTIN KERN**
(WWW.GARRETTKERN.COM)

Sauces, Dips, Etc.

SPICY RAMP CHEESE DIP

Yields 4 cups

🍂 INGREDIENTS

4 tablespoons butter
1 clove garlic, chopped
4 tablespoons flour
1 cup milk
8 ounces very sharp cheddar cheese, grated
1 can (10 ounces) Ro-Tel (Original with tomato and green chilies)
6–8 fresh ramps, finely chopped (leaf greens and white part)
⅓ cup pale ale beer (drink what's left)
Salt and pepper to taste
Hot sauce (optional)

🍂 DIRECTIONS

Over medium heat, melt butter in medium-sized saucepan. Add garlic and sauté lightly. Whisk in flour and continue to stir until this bubbles a little. Add milk and continue to stir until the sauce thickens.

Add the grated cheese and stir to melt. Add Ro-Tel, ramps and beer, and heat until dip is combined well and heated through.

Taste dip and add salt and pepper if needed. If you like it spicier, add a dash or two of hot sauce.

Serve hot with corn chips, pour over a nacho platter or baked potatoes.

RECIPE BY **LAURIE LITTLE**, WHITE GRASS CAFÉ, CANAAN VALLEY, WV

SIMPLE CRAB/RAMP DIP

🍂 **INGREDIENTS**

2 packages Louis Kemp (or other) imitation crab
1 small bunch ramps, washed, roots removed
1 package (or small tub) Philadelphia Cream Cheese
1 cup Hellmann's® Mayonnaise

2 tablespoons Worcestershire sauce, more or less to taste
1 box Keebler Club crackers

🍂 **DIRECTIONS**

Dice imitation crab into small pieces.

Dice fresh ramps, using white stem and at least 2 inches of the green lower leaf. If you have baby ramps, include the entire leaf.

Soften cream cheese in a good size bowl at room temperature and then combine with the mayo and Worcestershire sauce by hand whipping with a dinner fork. Add diced crab and ramps and blend with fork until evenly mixed. I told you that was simple!

Note: The diced ramp leaf provides a nice color to the mix. Larger late-season ramp leaves may be bitter, so use only the lower 2 inches. Increase or reduce quantity of ramps to taste.

DO NOT SCRIMP ON THE QUALITY OF THE CRACKER! The cracker is the delivery system to the palate, so choose your favorite cracker for this dish and stick to it. I prefer the Keebler Club because of its buttery taste and it holds up well to this stiff dip. Enjoy!

RECIPE BY **GHOST**, NORTHERN MICHIGAN

RAMP & ARUGULA PESTO

When I first made this pesto a few years ago my husband took one taste of the simple pasta tossed with it and wouldn't stop talking about how amazing it was. Prior to that if I had ever suggested just pasta, with no meat for dinner, he'd turn his nose up. Not with this pesto. So I make sure to make extra and fill ice cube trays with the sauce, freeze them and when they're nice and solid toss them in freezer bags, so I have nice individual 2 tablespoon servings for all kinds of uses.

Yields ¾ cup

INGREDIENTS

⅓ cup pine nuts
1 cup baby arugula
1 cup ramp greens, sliced
5 ramp bulbs, sliced
⅓ cup or more extra virgin olive oil
½ cup grated Parmesan
Sea salt and fresh cracked black pepper

DIRECTIONS

Gently toast the pine nuts in a small sauté pan over medium heat. Let cool.

In the food processor, whir the pine nuts, arugula, ramp greens and ramp bulbs until they are all chopped up.

While the processor is running, stream in the extra virgin olive oil; you may need more or less depending on how loose you want your pesto.

Finally, pulse in the Parmesan cheese. Taste and adjust the seasoning with salt and pepper.

Toss with fettucine, or add to a pizza, grilled chicken or fried potatoes.

RECIPE AND PHOTO BY **JEN HOFFMEISTER**, *PICCANTE DOLCE* BLOG
(HTTP://PICCANTEDOLCE.BLOGSPOT.COM)

RAMPS MAYONNAISE

Yields ¾–1 cup

⌀ INGREDIENTS

4–5 ramp bulbs, finely chopped
¼ teaspoon salt, plus more to taste
1 tablespoon ground horseradish powder (or mustard powder)
1 tablespoon vinegar
2 egg yolks
½ cup extra-virgin olive oil

⌀ DIRECTIONS

Combine chopped ramp bulbs with ¼ teaspoon salt and horse-radish powder, and crush to a paste in a mortar and pestle (or use food processor). Whisk in vinegar and egg yolks. Pouring the extra-virgin oil in a thin stream, whisk the mixture until achieving the consistency of mayonnaise. Season with more salt if necessary. Chill.

Use as you would conventional mayonnaise.

Photo at right shows Natasha's brie truffled burger with Kumato tomatoes and ramps mayonnaise.

RECIPE AND PHOTO BY **NATASHA PRICE**, *5-STAR FOODIE* BLOG
(WWW.FIVESTARFOODIE.COM)

RAMP HUMMUS

We enjoy this with toasted pita or pita chips. It's great as a dip with raw veggies, too.

Yields 1½ cups

～ INGREDIENTS

    1 can (15–16 ounces) garbanzo beans
      (reserve 1–2 tablespoons liquid)
    4 ramp bulbs
    ½ teaspoon cayenne pepper
    Juice of 1 lemon
    Kosher salt and fresh pepper, to taste
    2 tablespoons extra-virgin olive oil, for garnish
    1 ramp green top, finely sliced, for garnish

～ DIRECTIONS

In a food processor, purée all but the garnish. Add reserved liquid until you have your desired consistency. I usually add 1 tablespoon, as we like it thick.

Chill to let flavors meld.

Garnish the top with drizzled olive oil and the finely sliced ramp greens.

RECIPE BY **KURTIS UPTON**, WARREN, PA, ALLEGHENY HEIRLOOMS

Juice
& Jam

RAMP JAM
Ramps, sugar, water, vinegar, pectin
Use as relish and to make dip.
5 oz. net   (142 gms)

DELIGHTFUL RAMP TWIST

This is a vegetable and fruit drink with a delicious "something extra" provided by the ramps.

Yields approximately 2 cups

◈ INGREDIENTS

5 medium carrots
4 medium apples (tart variety is best)
2 large celery sticks, with the leaves
3–4 whole ramps, or just the bulbs (cleaned and de-rooted)
1 Key lime or ½ regular small lime, halved and then quartered

◈ DIRECTIONS

It is preferable to use organic or locally collected fruits and vegetables for your juice.

Wash and chop your fruits and vegetables to fit your juicer. Grind according to juicer instructions. Stir the juice when finished and enjoy.

RECIPE BY **MARILYNN CUONZO,** ELKINS, WV   PHOTO BY **AKIKO ENDO**

DOT MONTGILLION'S RAMP JAM

This same basic recipe is used to make other relish jams such as hot pepper jam and green pepper jam, but with different amounts of the "fruit."

Each early spring I make ramp jam and am sure other people have made it before me, since ramps are such a deeply ingrained tradition here in Appalachia. The "aroma" in preparing the ramp jam is the limiting factor as to how much jam I'm willing to make! So the first step in making ramp jam is to brace yourself for the smell of boiling ramps and resign yourself to a bath, shampoo and laundering your clothes afterwards! Now you are ready.

Yields approximately 12 half-pint jars

➤ INGREDIENTS

8 cups cleaned, chopped ramps, divided
  (use fully expanded plants, the green leaves and white bulbs)
3 cups white vinegar, divided
8 cups water, divided
1 teaspoon garlic powder, optional
2 boxes pectin (and 70% rubbing alcohol for pectin test)
10 cups sugar, plus more as needed

➤ DIRECTIONS

In a blender, add 4 cups ramps with 2 cups white vinegar, or enough to easily cover ramps, until a slurry is formed (the consistency of heavy cream). Add garlic powder for a boost of flavor. Repeat with 4 more cups of ramps, the remaining 1 cup vinegar and part of the water. Blend as before. Pour into a 3- or 4-gallon pot. Use remaining water to rinse the blender, and add that to the pot. Bring to a boil.

Add the pectin and bring to a hard boil. Do a pectin test: In a clear custard cup, add 3–4 drops of ramp mixture to 3 tablespoons 70% rubbing alcohol. If the mixture clots, there is enough pectin. (This test is valid for all jams and jellies.)

Add 10 cups granulated sugar. Stir until dissolved, and bring to a boil. Let boil at least 1 minute. Drop hot liquid from spoon. If drops tend to clump together, the jam is ready to pour into jars and seal. If liquid is still thin and watery, add more sugar, ½ cup at a time.

As you can see, jelly-making is still not entirely a science! I've been making jam/jelly most of my 83 years and I still am surprised from time to time!

RECIPE BY **DOT MONTGILLION**, WESTON, WV

PHOTO BY **HOLLY ROSBOROUGH**

Year-Round Ramps

A "NOSE-TO-TAIL" APPROACH
TO PRESERVING RAMPS

By Joel MacCharles

"They're very good but you threw out the best part." That was the reaction of a local chef who was sampling our first attempt at pickling ramps. We'd assumed that, like the "other" leek, the green could not be eaten and so we had destroyed the top of the plant. Considering the work that went into finding the ramps (at our hunting cabin, more than 10 miles from the nearest human), the news was sobering. This singular moment in my personal food history taught me more than almost any other experience.

Years later, I found myself absorbed by the approaches of Chef Fergus Henderson and many who followed his ideals of considering animals from nose-to-tail. My journey introduced me to Chef Mark Cutrara in Toronto who shared his experiences with me and that he wasn't a fan of many commercial cuts of meat which grouped two or more muscles in a single cut. He explained that each muscle was different and responded differently to cooking than the others.

Mixing my harsh lesson of wasting those ramp greens and the philosophy of nose-to-tail has transformed my approach to preserving fruit and vegetables. By treating the different parts differently you can bring the most out of each piece, which will extend the ability to use the flavors through the year. It is, indeed, nose-to-tail vegetables and fruits.

There are at least four edible parts of a ramp: the leaves, the bulb, the neck or hip, and the roots. It could be argued that the thick part of the stock between the bulb and leaf could be a fifth part but we haven`t treated it differently yet (though fermenting it or drying it and turning it into a powder for rubs would be my initial approach). Each is edible and each should be treated differently to maximize results.

❧

There are several preserving styles. Here are some of my favorites. You could take a single ramp and make all four of the following recipes, using a separate part for each.

DEHYDRATED RAMP ROOTS

These are fantastic with sashimi, seared fish or salads. Simply break off small pieces and scatter (or place a whole piece on your tongue and wait for 20–30 seconds and see how the taste progresses as the ramp becomes rehydrated in your mouth).

Cut roots from bulb, keeping a small piece of the bulb with the roots so that you keep the roots from each plant as a single unit. This will make them easier to handle and less likely to blow around in a dehydrator.

Wash the roots very well and remove any enzyme left from the bulb. Blanch quickly in boiling water (30 seconds), then plunge in an ice-water bath. This will speed up the drying time. Place in dehydrator at 125°F, until brittle. This will take 6–10 hours.

Store in an air-tight container like a mason jar with the lid on. If kept out of direct sunlight they should keep for a very long time.

DRYING THE BULB: SALT AND VINEGAR-STYLE RAMP CHIPS

Drying a single ingredient is a fine use for a dehydrator, but the technique leaves a lot of room for experimentation and cooking (really slowly). These chips are heavily seasoned with a savory vinegar and provide an amazing umami boost to any savory dish that needs it. The umeboshi vinegar comes from a Japanese plum and may turn your ramps a shade of purple, which is absolutely fine. (Note: the photo shows chips seasoned with a lighter vinegar.)

Using a mandoline, cut slices of the white part of your clean ramp. I do this directly over the tray that goes into my drier, which saves handling the delicate pieces later (a lesson learned the hard way). I use the mandoline with a great deal of care. Don't cut too finely as they will dry very thin (I cut at about 1/8-inch).

Spread the ramps out – they shouldn't touch or overlap. Complete for all trays before moving to next step.

Stack your trays over your sink. Splash vinegar on the top tray (you should hit most pieces, but don't worry about catching all of them). Season tray with fine salt (umeboshi is also salty, so you will want to account for that when deciding how much to use).

Move top tray to bottom of stack and repeat – it will gain more vinegar as you splash the other trays.

Dehydrate at 125°F. Time will vary depending on thickness – ours took about 8 hours.

INFUSING THE "NECK" OR "HIP": RAMP-INFUSED SHERRY VINEGAR

This couldn't be much simpler. It's a high-acid infusion, and it uses the part of the ramp between the bulb and the stem. Ideally, you'll want to use a 5% (or higher) vinegar. I stay away from heavier vinegar (like balsamic) or fruity (like cider), as I find they compete with the ramps. I've recently been infusing them in an aged sherry vinegar that's just lovely.

Take the clean necks of the ramps and put them in a bottle of sherry vinegar. Place cap on, or wrap with foil, and store in fridge for 2 weeks.

Use this vinegar in salad dressings or as you normally would in cooking. Use the "ramp bits" as you would use capers in other cooking. They are awesome chopped on pizza!

FREEZING THE LEAVES: BASIC PESTO FROM RAMP GREENS

Making pesto from ramp greens has been a subject of much debate in our family. For years we followed traditional recipes and added cheeses, nuts and oils from around the world. Recent years have me really appreciating the ramp for what it is, and I like to preserve it close to its original flavor – besides, you can add all that other stuff at the time of cooking (by keeping it simple when freezing you get more options later).

Place clean ramp leaves in a food processor. Give them a spin and reduce their volume for 10–15 seconds.

Add enough oil to transform the pieces of leaves into a paste. Any oil will do, though I prefer a mild vegetable oil. I try to stick to an oil from the area the ramps are from, out of a preference for the idea of terroir (we have great soya and canola oil from Ontario, as examples of what I'd use here where I live).

Season with salt to taste.

Pour single portions into muffin pan liners and freeze on a tray. Once frozen, place the pucks in bags in a freezer. You can use them a-puck-at-a-time in sauces, soups and stews through the year!

RECIPES AND PHOTOS BY **JOEL MACCHARLES** AND **DANA HARRISON**,
WELL PRESERVED BLOG

RAMP FESTIVALS AND EVENTS IN THE U.S. AND CANADA

Some of these annual events, big and small, have been going for up to 80 years. Most are in Appalachia, but new ones are starting up wherever ramps – a.k.a. wild leeks – are to be found, from Georgia to Ontario, Canada. Here is a partial list.

Eigensinn Farm's Wild Leek and Maple Syrup Festival – Singhampton, Ont., Canada; (519) 922-3128

Singhampton's Annual Ramp Romp – Singhampton, Ont., Canada; (705) 443-8007

Annual Ramp Fest Hudson – Hudson, NY; (518) 822-8938; rampfesthudson@gmail.com

Upper Delaware Valley Ramp Festival – Sullivan County, NY; (845) 482-5929

Annual Ramp Festival – Mt. Morris, PA; (304) 879-5500

VFW Post 6878 and Ladies Auxiliary Ramp Feed – Proctorville, OH; (740) 886-6219

Coolville Lions Club Ramp Dinner – Coolville, OH; (740) 667-6799

Harlan County Ridge Runners Annual Ramp Festival – Evarts, KY; jdjtroutman@windstream.net

Polk County Ramp and Tramp Festival – Greasy Creek, TN; (423) 338-4503

Flag Pond Ramp-Fest – Flag Pond, TN; (423) 743-6800; www.flagpond.com/festival/ramp/fest.htm

Annual Cosby Tennessee Ramp Festival – Cosby, TN; (423) 623-1009

Ramp Cook-Off – Swanton, MD; (301) 387-7067; (301) 387-7314

The Nestorville Ramp Dinner – Barbour County, WV; Sponsor: Kasson Ruritan Club

Tyler County FFA Annual Ramp Dinner – Middlebourne, WV; (304) 758-9000 Ext. 181

Buffalo Volunteer F. D. Ramp Dinner – Buffalo, WV; (304) 532-3380

Annual Upsher Co. Library Ramp Dinner – Buckhannon, WV; Library: (304) 473-4219 or (304) 472-4858; http://upshurcounty.lib.wv.us/friends.htm

Richwood Rampfest – Richwood, WV (the granddaddy of ramp festivals); (304) 846-6790; rwdchamber@richwoodwv.com

Delbert Baptist Church Annual Pine Knob Ramp Dinner – Norma, WV

Pickens Ramp Supper – Pickens, WV; (304) 924-5415

Camp Caesar Ramp Dinner – Camp Caesar, WV; (304) 226-3888; www.campcaesar.info/

Big Otter Ramp Feed – Big Otter, WV; (304) 286-2212

West Union Ramp Dinner – West Union, WV; (304) 266-9160

Quick Community Center Ramp Dinner – Pinch, WV; (304) 965-9008

Helvetia Ramp Dinner – Helvetia, WV; (304) 924-6435; (304) 924-5081; http://helvetiawv.com

Washington Bottom Ramp Feed – Wood County, WV; (304) 863-3311

Hacker Valley Ramp Dinners (two) – Webster County, WV; (304) 493-6488; (304) 493-6470

Roanoke Ramp Festival – Roanoke, WV; www.stonewallresort.com

Elkins International Ramps & Rails – Elkins, WV; (304) 636-4013

Bayard Volunteer F. D. Annual Ramp Dinner – Bayard, WV; (304) 693-7436

The Mt. Grove Volunteer F. D. Ramp Dinner – Eglon, WV; (304) 735-6801

The Reynoldsville Volunteer F. D. Ramp Dinner – Harrison County, WV; (304) 623-9309; (304) 745-5267

Faith Gospel Church Ramp Dinner – Parkersburg, WV; (304) 483-1079; www.faithgospelchurch.org/

Summers County Ramp Dinner – Hinton, WV; (304) 466-3220; www.hintonelks.com

Annual Williamsburg Ramp Dinner – Williamsburg, WV; (304) 645-6867; www.williamsburgwv.com

Springfield Volunteer F.D. Annual Ramp Dinner – Romney, Hampshire County, WV; (304) 492-5876

Frametown Volunteer F. D. Ramp Dinner – Frametown, WV; (304) 364-4094

Annual Ramp Dinner – Graysville, WV; (304) 845-0858

Ramp Dinner – Bomont, Clay County, WV; (304) 548-7101

Jenkins Chapel Annual Ramp Dinner – Mathias, WV;
(304) 897-8700

Ramps and Rainbow Festival – Cherokee, NC; (800) 438-1601,
general information for Cherokee

Bradshaw Volunteer F.D. Ramp Dinner – Green Mountain, NC;
(828) 688-9008

Chapter 29 of NC Eastern Star Ramp Dinner – Green Mountain,
NC; (828) 766-9719

West Burnsville Baptist Church Ramp Supper – Bakersville, NC;
(828) 682-3390

Ramp Dinner & Appalachian Dinner/Concert – Robbinsville, NC;
(828) 479-3364; info@StecoahValleyCenter.com

Buladean F.D. Ramp Dinner – Buladean, NC; (828) 688-4322

Waynesville Annual Ramp Convention – Waynesville, NC;
(828) 456-8691; (800) 334-9036

Cullasaja Gorge Fire & Rescue Annual Ramp Supper – Cullasaja,
Macon County, NC; (828) 369-5010

Whitetop Mountain Ramp Festival (Mt. Rogers VFD) –
Grayson County, VA; (304) 897-8700; (276) 388-3422

Ramp'n on the River Ramp Festival – Hiawassee, GA;
(706) 896-7400

SOURCES THAT WILL SHIP RAMPS TO YOU
(AND BULBS AND SEEDS)

If you don't live near an area where ramps grow, or you can't find ramps at your local farmers' market or greengrocer, you can have your spring fix anyway – by ordering directly and having them shipped.

Here are a few suppliers, to get you started:

☙ The Ramp Farm, Richwood, WV
"The only ramp farm in the world." Ramps are shipped the first three weeks of April by Priority Mail. You can order fresh ramps, as well as ramp seeds and ramp bulbs (planting instructions included). Bulbs are shipped late February or early March, depending on the weather.

www.rampfarm.com

Phone: (304) 846-4235

☙ Earthy Delights, DeWitt, MI
Earthy Delights is a leading supplier of specialty, wild-harvested and hand-crafted foods. They ship their fresh produce overnight to professional and at-home chefs across America. You can order whole ramps and ramp bulbs.

www.earthy.com

Phone: (800) 367-4709

Happy Cat Organics, Chester County, PA

Happy Cat sells fresh ramps and ramp seeds. They also sell 2-year-old ramp plants in 3.5-inch pots, ready to be planted in a light woodland location. They ship late April-early May.

www.happycatorganics.com; and
www.localharvest.org/ramps-wild-leeks-C8357
Phone: (610) 217-7723

Allegheny Heirlooms, Warren, PA

This CSA/family farm in northwest Pennsylvania ships wild leeks (ramps) harvested from carefully tended privately-owned land. To order small quantities sold by the pound (and various heirloom seeds year-round), e-mail to:

alleghenyheirlooms@rocketmail.com; and
crazychefkurtis@yahoo.com

Oregon Mushrooms, Keno, OR

They sell frozen ramp bulbs year-round. This is also a good source for truffles, sea salts and a wide assortment of mushrooms. They ship overnight via FedEx.

www.oregonmushrooms.com
Phone: (541) 882-3687; (800) 682-0036 (outside of Oregon)

The West Virginia Blogger

Fresh-foraged West Virginia mountain ramps are vacuum packaged and shipped Priority Mail.

www.bloggingwv.com/wild-ramps-for-sale/

ACKNOWLEDGMENTS

$\mathcal{T}$his book wouldn't be possible without the creativity and generosity of these far-flung members of our informal "Ramps Nation": the passionate chefs, food writers, bloggers and just plain wonderful folks who so kindly shared their favorite ramp recipes with us.

Winnie Abramson, Healthy Green Kitchen blog
(www.healthygreenkitchen.com)

Chef Bob Adkins, FARMbloomington, Bloomington, IN

Chef Mario Batali (www.mariobatali.com)

Julie Brady (Jaguar Julie), (www.squidoo.com/lensmasters/jaguarjulie)

Joanne Bruno, Eats Well With Others blog
(www.joanne-eatswellwithothers.com)

Jamie Carlson, You Have To Cook It Right blog
(http://youhavetocookitright.blogspot.com)

Adeline Cheng, My Kind Of Food blog
(http://mykindoffood.blogspot.com)

Michael Cirino and Linda Lou, a razor a shiny knife
(www.arazorashinyknife.com)

Giff Constable, Constable's Larder blog (www.constableslarder.com)

Marilynn Cuonzo, Elkins, WV

David Eger, Earthy Delights blog (www.earthydelightsblog.com)

Cathy Elton, What Would Cathy Eat blog
(www.whatwouldcathyeat.com)

Glen Facemire, The Ramp Farm, Richwood, WV
(www.rampfarm.com)

Ghost, Belluh's Run Farm, Northern Michigan

Chef Todd C. Gray, Equinox and Watershed restaurants,
Washington, D.C.

Jen Hoffmeister, Piccante Dolce blog
(http://piccantedolce.blogspot.com)

Matthew Kadey, Muffin Tin Mania blog (www.muffintinmania.com)

Garrett Kern, Garrett's Table blog (www.garrettkern.com)

Laurie Little, White Grass Café, Davis, WV

Kenji Lopez-Alt, Serious Eats blog (www.seriouseats.com)

Joel MacCharles and Dana Harrison, Well Preserved blog
(www.wellpreserved.ca)

Kathryn Matthews, Upstate Downtown blog
(https://upstatedowntownny.com)

Dot Montgillion, Weston, WV

Aimee Mott, co-author of The Fresh Dish blog
(www.thefreshdish.com)

Michael Natkin, Herbivoracious blog (www.herbivoracious.com)

Chef Chris Perkey, Iron Restaurant, Grand Rapids, MI

Kaela Porter, Local Kitchen blog (www.localkitchenblog.com)

Barbara Price, Greenwich Meal Time blog
(www.barbaraprice.wordpress.com)

Natasha Price, 5-Star Foodie blog (www.fivestarfoodie.com)

Archana Rao, Love Street Cakes; Don't F With Chef blog
(http://dontfwithchef.blogspot.com)

Rachel Rappaport, Coconut & Lime blog
(www.coconutandlime.com)

Maggie Raptis, Dog Hill Kitchen blog, (www.doghillkitchen.com)

Stephanie Russell, Okie Dokie Artichokie blog
(www.okiedokieartichokie.me)

Hank Shaw, Hunter Angler Gardener Cook blog
(www.honest-food.net)

David Turner and Danielle Sucher, Jack restaurant, NYC;
Habeas Brûlee blog (www.habeasbrulee.com)

Kurtis Upton, Allegheny Heirlooms
(alleghenyheirlooms2rocketmail.com and
krazychefkurtis@yahoo.com)

Chef Timothy Wastell, Firehouse Restaurant, Portland, OR

Most of the photographs were taken by the creators of the recipes, but we want to also acknowledge the images contributed by Alysin Bektesh, Akido Endo, Steph Goralnik, Herban Feast Catering, Justin Kern, Darya Pino, Holly Rosborough, J-P Thimot and Howard Walfish. Heartfelt thanks to everyone!!